Baby Animals in the Wild!

Zebra Foals in the Wild

by Marie Brandle

Bullfrog Books

Ideas for Parents and Teachers

Bullfrog Books let children practice reading informational text at the earliest reading levels. Repetition, familiar words, and photo labels support early readers.

Before Reading

- Discuss the cover photo. What does it tell them?

- Look at the picture glossary together. Read and discuss the words.

Read the Book

- "Walk" through the book and look at the photos. Let the child ask questions. Point out the photo labels.

- Read the book to the child, or have him or her read independently.

After Reading

- Prompt the child to think more. Ask: Zebra foals learn from their moms. What do they learn to do?

Bullfrog Books are published by Jump!
5357 Penn Avenue South
Minneapolis, MN 55419
www.jumplibrary.com

Library of Congress Cataloging-in-Publication Data

Names: Brandle, Marie, 1989– author.
Title: Zebra foals in the wild / by Marie Brandle.
Description: Minneapolis, MN: Jump!, Inc., [2023]
Series: Baby animals in the wild! | Includes index.
Audience: Ages 5–8
Identifiers: LCCN 2022010064 (print)
LCCN 2022010065 (ebook)
ISBN 9798885240833 (hardcover)
ISBN 9798885240840 (paperback)
ISBN 9798885240857 (ebook)
Subjects: LCSH: Zebra—Infancy—Juvenile literature.
Foals—Juvenile literature.
Classification: LCC QL737.U62 B73 2023 (print)
LCC QL737.U62 (ebook)
DDC 599.665/71392—dc23/eng/20220315
LC record available at https://lccn.loc.gov/2022010064
LC ebook record available at https://lccn.loc.gov/2022010065

Editor: Eliza Leahy
Designer: Molly Ballanger

Photo Credits: Danita Delimont/Shutterstock, cover; Pavel Kovacs/Shutterstock, 1; DaddyBit/iStock, 3; GranTotufo/Shutterstock, 4, 23tr; Keith 316/Shutterstock, 5, 23tm; Elliott Neep/Minden Pictures/SuperStock, 6–7; KenCanning/iStock, 8; Villiers Steyn/Shutterstock, 9, 23bl; Stu Porter/Shutterstock, 10; kjekol/iStock, 10–11; Simon Eeman/Shutterstock, 12–13, 23tl; JEAN-FR@NCOIS DUCASSE/Alamy, 14–15, 23bm; Petr Klimek/Alamy, 16–17; Victor1212/Shutterstock, 18; Stacey Ann Alberts/Shutterstock, 19; Anne Webber/Dreamstime, 20–21; Merrillie/iStock, 22; Maciej Czekajewski/Shutterstock, 23br; Palenque/iStock, 24.

Printed in the United States of America at Corporate Graphics in North Mankato, Minnesota.

Table of Contents

Brown Stripes

A herd of zebras lives on the savanna.

A foal is a baby.
It stays with Mom.

foal

Mom licks its fur.

Why?

This keeps it clean.

The foal has brown stripes.
They will turn black.

stripe

The foal has a mane.

mane

Look out!
A lion chases the herd.
The foal runs fast.
Its long legs help.

lion

The lion stops.

It can't see the foal.

Why?

Its stripes blend in.

The foal follows Mom.

It knows her stripes.

Each zebra has its own pattern!

They eat grass.
The foal learns where to find it.

It learns where to find water.

It drinks.

The zebras rest.

One watches for lions.

Sleep well!

Parts of a Zebra Foal

What are the parts of a zebra foal? Take a look!

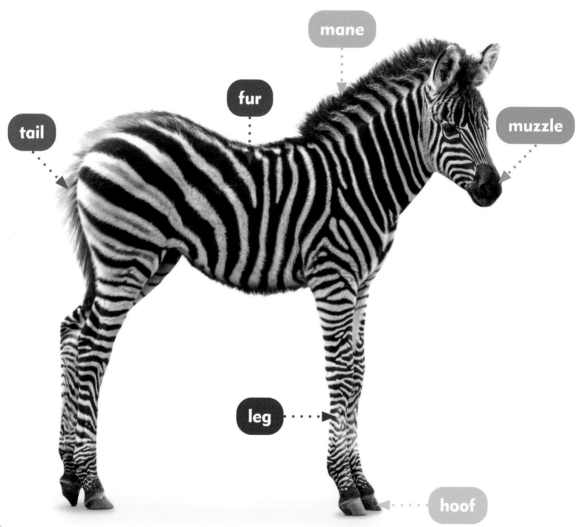

mane

fur

tail

muzzle

leg

hoof

Picture Glossary

blend in
To look like things nearby.

foal
A young zebra.

herd
A group of animals that stays or moves together.

mane
The thick hair on the head and neck of some animals.

pattern
A repeating arrangement of colors, shapes, or figures.

savanna
A flat, grassy plain with few or no trees.

Index

To Learn More

Finding more information is as easy as 1, 2, 3.

❶ Go to www.factsurfer.com

❷ Enter "zebrafoals" into the search box.

❸ Choose your book to see a list of websites.